Award-Winning Poems from the Smith's Tavern Poet Laureate Contest

2011 Edition

Compiled by the
Sunday Four Poets
Voorheesville, NY

SQUARE CIRCLE PRESS
VOORHEESVILLE, NY

Award-Winning Poems
from the
Smith's Tavern Poet Laureate Contest
2011 Edition

Published by
Square Circle Press LLC
137 Ketcham Road
Voorheesville, NY 12186
www.squarecirclepress.com

Printed in the United States of America on acid-free, durable paper.
ISBN-10: 0-9833897-7-2
ISBN-13: 978-0-9833897-7-4

Publisher's Acknowledgments
Special thanks to Edie Abrams, Michael Burke, and Dennis Sullivan of Sunday Four Poets for coordinating this publication project and providing the introductory information. Cover design by Square Circle Press; cover images provided by Richard Vang and Dataflow. Interior photographs by Saul and Edie Abrams.

"Evolution", "Winter Wren" and "Three Jokes for Science" by Howard Kogan were previously published in *Indian Summer* (Square Circle Press, 2011). An earlier version of "Tally" by Therese Broderick was previously self-published as "Safety in Numbers" in *At April's End* (2011). "Her Voice—A Japanese Haibun" by Stephen Leslie was previously published by *Contemporary Haibun Online* (June 2009). "Arlington" by Melinda Morris Perrin was previously published in *Winterberries: Poems of Hope* (Ice Cube Press, 2011).

Further acknowledgments from the Sunday Four Poets appear elsewhere in this book.

Contents

Contest organizers Dennis Sullivan, Edie Abrams, and Michael Burke. Photo by Saul Abrams.

Barn Owl Blues featuring Brenda Fisher and Ron Whitford entertained the gathering with music and song at halftime during the contest. Photo by Saul Abrams.

Sunday Four Poets
Acknowledgments

The Sunday Four Poets would like to express our deepest thanks to the following whose help and assistance assured a much talked about, successful, second annual Smith's Tavern Poet Laureate Contest.

Jon McClelland and John Mellen, proprietors of Smith's Tavern in Voorheesville, who sponsored the event and made the restaurant available as the venue for the contest.

Jill, Audrey, Carol, and Kathy, the efficient and friendly wait staff at Smith's Tavern.

Paul Amidon, Suzanne Fisher, Tim Verhaegen, and Barbara Vink, who served as the panel of judges for the 2011 contest.

Georgia Gray, scorekeeper for the 2011 contest.

Saul Abrams, troubleshooter, photographer, and floor-walker during the 2011 contest.

Barn Owl Blues featuring Brenda Fisher and Ron Whitford, who provided musical entertainment at halftime during the 2011 contest.

Elliott Horvath and Dataflow, for the bookmarks, event posters, and image of the scroll on the cover.

Melissa Hale-Spencer and the staff of *The Altamont Enterprise*, who provided pre- and post-event coverage.

Richard Vang of Square Circle Press, for his enthusiasm and work in bringing forth this publication.

All of the contestants and their supporters, who provided a fun-filled, entertaining, and meaningful afternoon of laureate poetry at Smith's Tavern.

Your Sunday Four Hosts,

Edie Abrams, Michael Burke, Dennis Sullivan

Displayed amidst copies of the 2010 edition of this book is the coveted Poet Laureate trophy of William Shakespeare. Photo by Saul Abrams.

Smith's Tavern in Voorheesville provided a warm and welcoming atmosphere for the poets and their supporters. Photo by Saul Abrams.

About the Sunday Four Poets and
Smith's Tavern Poet Laureate Contest

Despite the wonderfully varied, colorful, and hospitable poetry open mics that abound in the cities of Albany, Schenectady, Troy (coming soon), and Saratoga Springs—which we attend whenever the opportunity arises—we had a hunch that a new and slightly-different venue was called for to celebrate the bardic work of the Flatlanders of Voorheesville and their neighbors situated high up in the Hilltowns of Albany County.

We wanted a venue set not in the evening or during the week but on a lazy Sunday afternoon between late breakfast and early dinner when the day offered time for thinking and reflection. We wanted as well this open mic to be grounded in the existing arts culture of our town. Hence we were thrilled when Andy Spence of Old Songs welcomed us to use the Old Songs Community Arts Center in Voorheesville as our home base. It is such a comfortable and hospitable space; we are honored to share in the great tradition of Old Songs.

We also wished to create a showcase in the form of a competition during which our area poets could pit their best work against the best work of their colleagues, the way the great dramatists Aeschylus and Sophocles vied against each other in 5th-century Greece. Thus in April 2010 we saw life given to the First Annual Smith's Tavern Poet Laureate Contest, considered by all far and wide in every respect to be a grand success.

The poems presented in this *libellum* are those of the 2011 Laureate (Howard Kogan), the Second Place poet (Marilyn Paarlberg), and the poet who received Honorable Mention (obeedúid~). Poems from other contestants are also included in this edition.

On Sundays when we do meet, now in our third season, it is heartening to see such attentive ears working to grasp the finely-crafted lines of the presenting poets who gather at Sunday Four, and to see faces light up even more when we gather afterward at the "Poets' Corner" at Smith's Tavern to continue our forays into *ars poetica*.

Voorheesville has a fine tradition of residents bringing together friends infused with a thirst for the arts dating back to the Bay View Club established by May Daring, Lavinia Joslin, and Mary Vosburgh in October of 1904. Here in our monthly open mic at Old Songs we celebrate our connection to this history by giving voice to the increasingly fine and commanding work of our regional poets.

Your Sunday Four Hosts,

Edie Abrams, Michael Burke, Dennis Sullivan

The 2011 contest judges (from left): Barbara Vink (2010 Poet Laureate), Suzanne Fisher, Paul Amidon, and Tim Verhaegen. Photo by Saul Abrams.

The diligent scorekeeper for the 2011 contest, Georgia Gray. Photo by Edie Abrams.

2011
Smith's Tavern Poet Laureate Contest Rules

Cash Prizes: Poet Laureate - $100 & name inscribed on trophy displayed at Smith's tavern; Runner-up - $50; Honorable Mention - $25.

Terms: Open to the first twenty-five poets who registered by email, beginning at Noon on March 31, 2011. Email submissions must have been from the poet themselves. No walk-ins on the day of the contest.

Alternates: No alternates were allowed for the twenty-five poets selected. A no-show resulted in disqualification.

Reading Guidelines: Each poet read three poems (one per round) of under 25, 35, and 45 lines respectively. Only lines of text were counted; titles or blank lines of numbers or letters setting off stanzas were not counted. Poet read their poems once only, without introductory comments. Poets whose poems exceed the maximum number of lines for that round were disqualified.

Reading Schedule: Poets were randomly assigned a reading order by round beforehand. There were two opening rounds, followed by a 40-minute break, then the final round. There was a brief break between readings for judges to tabulate their scores. Prizes were awarded immediately following the readings.

Judging Criteria: Presentation of the poem was to be clear and understandable, conveyed awareness, and had good flow, rhythm and tempo. Mechanics of the poem must have employed metaphor and imagery, exhibit concision and wholeness, and have good sound. The depth of feeling must have been unique, creative, passionate, inspirational, fresh and thoughtful. The overall impact must have been engaging, interesting, stimulating, captivating, and compelling. In the event of tie, the judges' scores with the lowest total score for each tied poet was to be dropped, and repeated until the tie was broken.

Judges: Paul Amidon, Suzanne Fisher, Tim Verhaegen, Barbara Vink.

Scorekeeper: Georgia Gray.

Hosts: Edie Abrams, Michael Burke, Dennis Sullivan.

Award-Winning Poems
from the
Smith's Tavern
Poet Laureate Contest

2011 Edition

Howard Kogan reads during the 2011 contest. Photo by Saul Abrams.

Howard J. Kogan

Howard J. Kogan is a social worker/psychotherapist who lives with his wife Libby in the Taconic Mountains, where he enjoys rural life and writing. About his writing he states, "After setting aside writing poetry in my twenties to attend to the concerns of family and work, I returned to it in my sixties. I have been fortunate to have this opportunity to return to an early love. I think of it as an Indian summer, a season of sun and tranquility nestled between the foreshadowing of what's to come and its final arrival." His first collection of poems, *Indian Summer*, was published by Square Circle Press in 2011.

The 2011 Poet Laureate with John Mellen and Jon McClelland of Smith's Tavern. Photo by Saul Abrams.

Howard J. Kogan
Evolution

*"Homo sapiens are a tiny twig on an improbable branch of
a contingent limb on a fortunate tree." (Stephen Jay Gould)*

What Homo sapiens would believe such a thing?

In our heart of hearts we know
the first blue-green bacterium flipped
their little riboswitches and knitted
their strands of nucleotides dreaming of us.

Didn't the first paramecium point its microscopic
snout and twitch its cilia to hula over to us?
Just as the first amoeba stretched a shapely pseudopod
to tango in our direction?

In time they all found themselves in the Garden of Eden.
Looking up, as Adam and Eve looked down, admiring
their perfect reflection in the pond's mirrored surface.
It was at this moment on the spiral staircase of evolution

certainty begot doubt. The little strivers in the pond wondered
if perhaps they should've aimed at something less multi-cellular.
Wondered if it might still be possible to re-direct creation
toward sponges or perhaps fish.

Wondered if it might still be possible to snip
this twig before the awful weight of its self-
importance caused it to fall — carrying
the rest of creation with it.

Howard J. Kogan
Winter Wren

Received this morning, one winter wren,
a gift from Tux, our cat, who found it hopping
on the ground in the front garden like a vole,
which is what I thought it was,
and, to be frank, slowed my rescue.

When I called Tux, he left it,
but then, as though remembering
his manners, returned to fetch it in.
A last minute offering, the way you,
a person of good manners, might stop
at an all-night drugstore to pick up
a hostess gift after an impromptu
dinner invitation. Though none
was expected or needed.

So it was my fate to hold the tiny wren
through its final tremor and twitch,
its wiry legs pedaling slowly until it lay
loose-headed in the manner of the dead.
Its chestnut feathers lifting
at the final moment, as if something
was released, and then subsiding
as the checker-spotted breast stilled.

This poem is her epitaph.
Let the universe take note
of the loss of one young winter
wren, who died in my hand
while the ever hopeful Tux,
purred with pleasure,
and graciously waited,
for me to eat it.

Howard J. Kogan
Three Jokes for Science

When I was eight, an older boy
told me our town's two large
supermarkets, Stop and Shop and A & P
were merging to became Stop & P.
It was the high point of my first decade.
It still rates a smile in my seventh.
Which may be more evidence than I really want
that while youth is fleeting, immaturity is forever.

In my twenties there was the one
about the Englishman.
I confess I went through a phase
of loving everything English.
This may account for my affection,
for the Englishman who wore two monocles,
and made a spectacle of himself.

In my thirties there was the story
about this fellow who goes to Miami
for his annual vacation.
He sees a beautiful woman
in his hotel lobby and winks.
She whispers, "I'm selling."

He whispers, "I'm buying."
A few weeks later he's at the doctor's
and learns he has gonorrhea.
The next year, it's the same week,
the same hotel, the same woman.
She whispers, "I'm selling."
He whispers, "What are you selling this year —
kidney stones?"

You may be asking,
"How are three old jokes a poem?"
Don't ask. Actually I am conducting
a scientific experiment,
involving all the dead poets,
from Gilgamesh in the Twentieth Century BC
to Ginsberg in the Twentieth Century AD.

The experiment theorizes this poem
will cause forty centuries of dead poets
to spin in their graves with enough velocity
to spark a few new ideas.
The ideas we have now aren't working.

Marilyn Paarlberg reads during the 2011 contest. Photo by Saul Abrams.

Marilyn Paarlberg

Marilyn Paarlberg lives and writes in a drafty old farmhouse outside of Albany, and wouldn't have it any other way.

The 2011 Runner-up with Jon McClelland of Smith's Tavern. Photo by Saul Abrams.

Marilyn Paarlberg
Biker

Jesus ripples on the left deltoid
while the Blessed Virgin dotes
from her latissimus dorsi grotto.
Coiled on the iliac, the serpent
licks his lips at Eve
seductively splayed
from trapezius down
to where she teases
a bulging gluteus maximus
with her bare toes.
Kept at arm's length,
Mother shrinks into her heart
on the right biceps.
All of them sweating —
unaccustomed to muscling
with a mixed crowd.

Marilyn Paarlberg
Late for Work, New Bird at the Feeder

Our alarm overslept.
Startled by silence
you remember you forgot
to pick up a pound
of the humid Sumatran
we fume to find — sultry,
dark as last night when
coffee wasn't on our minds.

The shower takes up its task,
pummeling my back
with tunnels hot as I can stand.
You hand me a towel — not mine,
with a scent of aftershave
and the moist slope of your spine.

Awake.
I leave the starting gate,
pull a sweater over wet hair,
dash to the kitchen where
you're buttering toast.
Brush crumbs off your chest,
jam from my lip for a kiss to go.
A flutter at the window —
plump flit, cinnamon breast.

Marilyn Paarlberg
I Have her Rolling Pin

Pecan.
Rhubarb.
Berry.
Cream.
Apple,
peach,
lemon meringue,
Double crust, Dutch,
crackers, crumbs,
fluted, forked,
with sugared rims
cooling in windows,
as if to share first taste
with the hungry air.
I roll out these lines,
seasoned with sounds. Soft,
ripe words sliced for you,
lover of art. Part
of my gift is this poem
which lies light, then
melts to memory
like my mother's pies.

obeedúid~

obeedúid~, a/k/a Mark W. O'Brien, has been a member of The Every Other Thursday Night Poetry Group since the 1990s and participates in the Posey Cafe Study Group. obeedúid~ reads frequently at local poetry venues. He has published 12 books of poetry and numerous broadsides; three of which were published by Benevolent Bird Press. His poems have appeared in "Tin Wreath", "The Antediluvian Levee", "Many Waters", "Peer Glass An Anthology From Hudson Valley Peer Groups", "Poetry Don't Pump Gas: Every Other Thursday Night Poets", "Rootdrinker", "Normanskill", and the "Rootdrinker Anthology of Contemporary Poetry".

obeedúid~ has his own YouTube Channel: "Videobeedude!" where he produces VideO'ems and documents other local poets works and their readings. obeedúid~'s most recent collection of poems entitled "Neo-lethean Dreams" was published by Benevolent Bird Press in 2009. He is currently at work on a new collection of 30 Poems tentatively entitled: "Telluric Voices: Ut pictura poesis" intended for the E-book multimedia market with embedded VideO'ems.

An excerpt from his autobiography "Pneumatic Thoughtforms: The Strange Mythos Of How I came to be a Poet":

> *"When I was in the third grade I had a horrible time learning to read on the same level as my peers. I suppose I must have actually been an undiagnosed dyslexic. In desperation my parents began sending me to Maria Collage in Albany every weekend for an entire summer for special instruction with Sister Mother Mary Whatshername. Her method of teaching me to read consisted of repetitive phonics mixed with rhyming poetry. By the end of the summer I was hooked on phonics and poetry!"*

obeedúid~ lives loudly in the sleepy little hamlet of Clarksville, NY with his two children and poetically challenged pets.

*obeedúid~ reads during the 2011 contest.
Photo by Saul Abrams.*

*Dennis Sullivan of Sunday Four Poets announces the
2011 Honorable Mention as Jon McClelland of Smith's
Tavern awards the prize. Photo by Saul Abrams.*

obeedúid~
How the sky was emptied:

Remember the sun
the flaming ball of heaven
how it seemed reachable
when it rested on the hill
in the evening

Remember how
you climbed away
from your parents house
stumbling
crawling on all fours
your heart pounding with excitement
about to take the sun
in your hands

When finally
you pushed through
the nettles, goldenrod, scrub pine

there
the sun
calm, burning
but miles away

a valley between

Like the tedium children feel
waiting on adults
their life

suspended

obeedúid~
A Picture Of Your Parents Pitching Woo:

Can the casual incident
of someone's going
become the certain accident
that brought you forth?

Can you know
they took this path
on that day
after they married?

Here
is the amber photograph
to prove it
charged with static
rubbing against memory.

The wind in their hair
as they strode along
the glow of walking
on their faces.

If they had not lingered
you might not be
you would have remained
in nothingness.

Perhaps
the sea glittered
pewter and blue
along that path
the day you were conceived.

How soft on the face
wind from the sea
an amorous gesture
that brought you forth.

obeedúid~
... into a small dark space:
(For Steve Dudek)

I'm thinking
of sardines again
how the world changes
how things get lost
from our lexicon.

Like herring in a barrel
becomes
like sardines in a can.

They stopped using barrels
now
they no longer can sardines.

In my hometown
at the local methodist church
every sunday night
we've been playing
a version of hide & seek
called "sardines"
for as long
as they've packed
fish in a can.

This year
we had to explain
what a sardine is.

Why
when you pile
into a small dark space
in some dusty hideaway
where no one goes
it is like fish
packed tightly
in a can.

Then
the thought occurred to me:

"What would we call this game
  without a reference point?"
Can we find something new
that recovers our loss?

I'm thinking
of sardines again
how the world changes
how things get lost
from our lexicon.

The 2011 prize winners. Photo by Saul Abrams.

Competitor Submissions

In this, our second year of the Smith's Tavern Poet Laureate Contest and subsequent commemorative book, the Sunday Four Poets thought we would include one poem from each participant. Though the poets are presented here in the order that they read during the Third Round of the competition, the poems presented are a poem of poet's choice, and not necessarily the specific poem that the poet read during that round. The intent is to show the full, rich spectrum of poems presented during the contest, and hopefully to encourage new and returning poets to participate in the third Smith's Tavern Poet Laureate Contest in April 2012.

The poets who participated in the 2011 Smith's Tavern Poet Laureate Contest. Photo by Saul Abrams.

Therese Broderick
Tally

The 6am news gives the latest tally of dead and wounded.
For the rest of the day, I seek safety in numbers.

At breakfast I rescue raisins from a bowl of cereal.
With a sterling spoon, I lift two-by-two out of muddy

flakes, transfer them to a clean white saucer. When done
I count again just to be sure: yes, all 10 made it out.

Later I sort laundry. I search for my daughter's socks
camouflaged against flannel pajamas. I peel apart

each clinging foot, find its mate, fold one into the other,
build a stockpile of bundled cotton. 24 socks, a dozen pairs.

After lunch the mail comes. Some of it is junk, but today
I will not mutilate plastic windows nor discard anything

unread. I handle each piece as though a telegram to a
soldier's mom, unsealing 8 flaps, whispering every line.

By half past 5 my daughter and husband are done with work
and come to eat. We hold hands, recite together

our 11 words, 30 consonants, 16 vowels, 14 syllables:
We give thanks for our plenty when others have so little.

D. Colin
Inauguration

He ran his campaign in my heart
so I would vote for him
when it came election time.
Despite the negative
advertisements I dismissed
as the competition's attempt to prevent
love from happening,
I registered
only to find the truth in his politics was
faulty in false promises ...
but I still let him run his term
until I realized my vote
never really mattered
until I learned he was never
worthy of my government.
I rioted and planned
a coup d'etat to repossess my Queendom.
He accused me of anarchy after I impeached him.
I laughed
No longer susceptible to empty speeches
ready to live again
inaugurating myself
into a future without him.

Carolee Sherwood
The kind of clever darkness we're up against

Three flocks of blackbirds hurry over the bridge.
They carry the final puzzle pieces of night in their beaks,
put them in place above the Hudson River.

This is the kind of clever darkness we're up against.
Cold infiltrates our streets, our walls, our pipes,
sneaks through windows, stuffs itself in sidewalk seams.

The barks of your neighbor's dog freeze
the instant they leave his muzzle.
They pile up in the yard like snow banks.

Above, planes whoosh like sleds on metal runners.
January is leaving us without the thaw it promised,
and they're calling for an early February storm.

I can't ward off winter. Even in your bedroom,
frost laces pillowcases. Icicles fringe rugs.
The ceiling, vast glacier, intends to crush us.

We tremble in each others arms, light candles
on shelves and dressers, a circle of protective fires.
Before we close our eyes, we will have to blow them out.

This is the kind of clever darkness we are up against.

Stephen Leslie
Her Voice — A Japanese Haibun

Lacking social grace, she constantly interrupts my conversations with firm but clear directions. When I fail to make a critical turn in time, there are no judgments, no recriminations. She studies the maps and quickly computes a new route. She only speaks when necessary. Her voice, while feminine, is neither sexy nor nagging. During the long straight drives on the Interstate, she is content to be quiet. Speaking only when necessary. At the end of a long trip she guides me through the thick fog and haze, using her abilities to connect with an unseen higher power to guide us back home.

Sometimes I wish she was more cordial, but our relationship is all business. When it is time for us to part she is silent ... but I know I will hear her voice again.

Swirling dense fog
Her reassuring voice
GPS

Bob Sharkey
Freak Stone

A small rounded stone found me
seeking shells for Kathy's garden.
"Look for my sibs or at least
a cousin, won't you," stone begged.
Well, ok. Kept my head down
towards the dry debris line
of a few high tides ago
along Grand and then Pine Point
rolling stone in my pocket.
Didn't find another like it, granite,
gray like the undersides of empty clouds,
gray with faded black ring all around.
Nothing even close.
Found shells for Kathy.
Found a small quartz, lavender
like the evening sky there,
and a black oval basalt.
Found, cowled against the cold howl
and shaded from the bright sand,
other walkers, monk like,
within themselves, proclaiming nothing
and thus attracting the question,
"what stone are you rolling?"
Found that the stone that found me
had found me on a perfect day,
a day where no one special event occurred
but all went well, the world unreported,
the penultimate day and so the day
most appreciated at that place.

Scott Knox
Skip

A man made of wood he seems to be.
Visions of robots dance close to me.
Or was it a coal car run amuck,   a fence post,   a derrick,   lunatic stuff!

Now, Skip did have his furniture days. Odd cabinets, tall rockers, even a chaise.
Unfortunately, one chair got stuck in the floor and five-sided baubles crawled up on the door.
He tried to turn nice tools in a case. But, this dammed old beer keg just   snuck into place.
Then there was a fifties lunch table; wooden cup, spoon, and menu left by the waitress: Mabel.
And, no home could ever be complete without Skips' wooden urinal and toilet bowl seat.

With time and with grace it seems to me, Skip is turning to wood. ... Naturally.
But, why are these guys and gals standing around?
Are they here to worship and cherish Skips' ground? .... No.
Skip knew we had our own voice to sound.
He taught by example, not whips or a crown.
He gave us not a dogma to follow.
He knew art by imitation is shallow.
He steeped us in our own creative milieu,
letting our thoughts and feelings accrue.
He shared with us patience and good technique,
waiting for growth each semester's critique.

Years came and went.   New faces appeared,
asking for help from this man with a beard.
With pencil on ear and student in tow
Skip guided his ship with care this we know.
From these Friends-of-Wood both near and afar,
We say,   Thank You Skip, with respect beyond par.

Melinda Morris Perrin
Arlington

"I hate Red Ants!"
You said.
The words harsh and jarring
With more passion than I was accustomed to hearing
From your gentlemanly, North Carolina-tinged voice.

We continued to walk across the stunted grass that grows in Florida's sandy soil,
Avoiding the occasional mounds of offending insects,
And I waited for the story behind the words.

You didn't talk much about your experiences in Viet Nam,
But I knew a little about your history,
Your awards and commendations.
You were among the oldest helicopter pilots in combat,
Father to the young men.
Responsible.
Duty-bound.
You never talked about your bravery.
Your medals remained in a drawer.

"It was hot."
You said,
"I kept the chopper still and steady as we took enemy fire.
Slowly, one by one, we lifted the men off the hill.
The wounded came first. Covered with Red Ants.
Angry Red Ants that crawled over my body and bit and stung.
I kept that chopper still and steady till all the men were on-board."
"I hate Red Ants."
The words softer now.

Today I stand before the stone that bears your name
In the lush green grass of Arlington.
Eyes cast down, I look around.
Say a prayer.
Grateful that here, at least,
There are no Red Ants.

Tom Corrado
The Undoing of the Do-It-Yourselfer

Bespectacled crusaders against the weatherbeaten
against the inevitability of decline
the insistence of wear and tear, of demise, of oxidation
eschewing orange-aproned yeasayers
trafficking the intricacies of replacing a washer
in a drippy kitchen faucet, running numbers
on fixer-uppers with free tickets to after-hour haunts
where sequined curtains part for whisperers
filling in the blanks, you will be applauded
by the graffiti-stained, heralded by street corner profiteers
and by all members of the extended *familia*
your boats moored in the marina at *La Mancha*.
There is nothing left of the landscape
nothing left of the ideas that ballooned
above the congregation — the congregation that now
at a drop in the Dow scalps tickets
to sit at the feat of the next double header.
If you can drive a nail, fine; if not, *no problema*.
Browse YouTube, punch in your query
and be awash in multi-lingual, detailed instructions
for rehabbing your backyard gazebo for those —
and isn't that just about every one of us? —
who in a weakened weekend moment would pounce
on the tri-folded specs of the Gates of Hell
where, when summer begins to unravel —
as it most surely will — we will assemble, reassured
that in these dark days of terror-ists and global warnings,
every do-it-yourselfer will score a bogey
in view of no less than 10 neighbors
who moonlight as anonymous purveyors of blogspeak.

Therese Broderick

D. Colin

Carolee Sherwood

Stephen Leslie

Bob Sharkey

Scott Knox

Melinda Morris Perrin

Tom Corrado

Rachael Z. Ikins

Frank S. Robinson

Susan Oringel

Photos of
participating poets
by Saul Abrams.

Rachael Z. Ikins
Army Lay-over, Winter Night, France

Definition, Phillip's death. Like I must've had hope, all these years.
As if I'd continued to look for him in all the wrong people.
As if the love we once had was *brilliant*. Like the stars in work you see
on posters, mugs, tee-shirts, *brilliant*, enough to light my path
til the end of my days, but I only just understand this now.

Pointlessly, I try to write poetic impressions about the night in '45
he was with the army encamped over Provençe hillsides.
Commander found him, 17 yrs. old. "I heard you know how.
Can you make enough for everyone?" The question. The story.
"My father taught me. I thought all 12 year old boys made
this dessert for their parents' dinner parties."

British soldiers rustling up cast iron fry pans, peasants
who lived nearby lifted floor boards, offered hoarded butter,
precious flour, eggs, cognac's eye-watering perfume; guys from Indiana,
Bristol, Oregon, guys who spoke no English, under night-sky's pinwheels, crêpes suzette
for hundreds. Small fires twinkled like diamonds inside circlets of lonely men.
Cigarettes winked, fire-flies. I gave up on the poem. It was the word
"fire-flies." I dreamt of him the next 2 nights in a row. I reached for him,
touched his skin near a shoulder-blade, his neck, his silver curls. He used to use
Brillcreme. Never knew a man outside TV who did, washed his hair with Ivory soap, an
army hold-over. He always smelled good. His scent lingered for years on my fingers.

Next night's dream, he instructed me, sotto voce, how to survive …
He said, "That's okay, just do it." An explanation. One of his expressions "Do it
anyway." He wore the navy Pierre Cardin suit I bought him, white St. Laurent shirt
beneath, navy Bucks, matching pocket square and silk tie, his second pair of tortoise-
shell-framed glasses, the pair he accidentally lost in the dish-washer or the freezer on his
way to surgical rounds. After that dream, I started to look forward to night, but since his
last comment, no word. He died June 1 @ 9:45 p.m. in a small Texas
town. The death certificates appeared in my mailbox after a birthday afternoon swimming
at my mother's house, eating chocolate cake filled with raspberry jam.
He endured cancer. In the end his heart simply stopped.
I walk over to look at the marked-up calendar on my fridge,

page back a month. It was a Tuesday. I try to recall what exactly
absorbed me, at that time, on that night, my unawareness
of his dying, we were once that close.

Frank S. Robinson
Light

I said, "Let there be light,"
And lifted my finger —
While other men, far distant,
Flexed muscles shined with sweat,
Digging the depths to claw out ore,
That others still would take and smelt
In blazing furnace caverns,
To make the iron rails, laid down
With hammers, spikes and blood,
From mountains to the sea,
Upon which run the fire-breathing trains,
Hauling their loads that other men
Have drilled and mined and died
To make the Earth yield up,
The black remains of ancient life,
Tons and barrels hoisted onto freight cars,
Sped along those rails to other halls of fire,
Cathedrals flaming and roaring,
Where the heat of the Sun itself,
That burned ten million years ago,
Is stoked by other men to burn anew
Into a hurricane of boiling steam
That spins a turbine in magnetic coils,
Driving invisible electrons,
Like buffalo stampeded,
Not off a cliff but through miles of wire,
Held aloft by gleaming giants built of steel,
Marching across the horizon,
To deliver those thunderbolts to where
My lifted finger touched the switch,
And there was light.
And it was good.

Susan Oringel
Olive Juice

I love alliteration's tricky licks and the *ahs*
of assonance — time to relax — delicious
fricatives and glottal stops. The blunt
flat hammers of *stab* and *shit*!
Those Anglo-Saxons really knew their,
er, stuff, and the polysyllabic latinates
aren't too shabby, either. But rhyme
that chimes, *Ay, ay, ay,* some
subtlety, puhleeeez! And it
amuses me how love and loathe
are close, in sound, anyway,
how "olive juice" said to someone
across a room sounds like "I love you."
Try it. And no matter how nicely someone
says my full first name, it always
sounds like Mother yelling.

Award-Winning Poems from the

Smith's Tavern Poet Laureate Contest

2010 Edition

compiled by Sunday Four Poets

Each year in April the poets of New York's Capital Region make their annual pilgrimage to Voorheesville, a quiet upstate village nestled among the shadows of the Helderberg Escarpment in western Albany County. They are inspired by the quest to have their name engraved upon the coveted trophy of William Shakespeare given to the poet crowned as Laureate of Smith's Tavern. The contest, a rousing success since its inception, is organized by the Sunday Four Poets, an open-mic poetry forum dedicated to continuing the rich cultural legacy of Voorheesville and the adjacent hilltowns.

ISBN: 978-0-9789066-9-6
$9.95

Indian Summer

poems by Howard Kogan

Howard J. Kogan began writing poetry in his twenties, but set it aside to pursue family life and a career as a social worker and psychotherapist. In his sixties he returned to writing poetry, a time he wistfully refers to as his "Indian summer." In 2011, Howard was named Poet Laureate of Smith's Tavern, an annual contest held in Voorheesville featuring the top poets of New York's Capital Region. This first collection of fifty poems includes the six he submitted for the 2010 and 2011 Smith's Tavern contests.

ISBN: 978-0-9833897-3-6
$12.95

AVAILABLE AT WWW.SQUARECIRCLEPRESS.COM

CPSIA information can be obtained at www.ICGtesting.com
Printed in the USA
BVOW071203061111

275344BV00001B/27/P